Better Mousetraps

Better Mousetraps

Product Improvements
That Led to Success

by Nathan Aaseng

Lerner Publications Company
Minneapolis

Page one: Eastman Kodak Company founder George Eastman (left) and inventor Thomas Edison were friends and collaborators. Edison used the idea of Kodak's continuous roll of film when he invented his first motion picture camera.

Page two: Pepperidge Farm founder Margaret Rudkin inspects loaves of bread in the cooling room. Bread is cooled for two hours before it is packaged.

Library of Congress Cataloging-in-Publication Data

Aaseng, Nathan.
   Better mousetraps: product improvements that led to success / by Nathan Aaseng.
      p. cm.
   Includes bibliographical references.
   Summary: Presents brief biographies of individuals who improved, refined, and perfected various products and processes, from cameras to razors.
   ISBN 0-8225-0680-7 (lib. bdg.)
   1. New products—United States—History. 2. Success in business—United States—History. I. Title.
HF5415.153.A23   1990   89-12803
658.5′75—dc20   CIP

Manufactured in the United States of America

2 3 4 5 6 7 8 9 10 99 98 97 96 95 94 93

To Bill and Dorothy

Contents

Improvements in the typewriter led to a successful line of typewriting equipment for Remington Arms Co.

Introduction

BEING FIRST MAY BE IMPORTANT IN races and in record books, but it is not a guarantee of success in the business world. One example of this truth involved the typewriter. Philo Remington is credited with producing the first successful commercial typewriting machine. Yet he was a Johnny-come-lately in the business, a gunsmith who probably would have had nothing to do with typewriters if he had not had a reputation for making precision parts.

The first patent for a typewriting machine was issued in 1714 to Englishman Henry Mill, more than a century before Remington was born. At least 51 other versions were patented by hopeful inventors during the next century and a half, but none were sold successfully.

In the 1860s, a newspaperman, Christopher Sholes, developed his own typewriter, which had letters of type on the ends of long metal arms arranged in a semicircle.

Unfortunately, the machines produced by Sholes's company kept breaking down. After three-fourths of the typewriters were returned for repairs, Shole sought help from the Remington Arms Co.

The Remington Arms Co. had expanded from its origins as a weapons manufacturer into making precision parts for a number of companies. In 1873, Remington introduced a redesigned version of Sholes's invention, complete with a foot treadle to return the carriage. The Remington typewriter was so much better than other typewriters that it enjoyed almost immediate success. It became a leader in the industry and has remained a popular brand to this day.

Philo Remington

This story illustrates the wisdom of a bit of advice most frequently credited to Ralph Waldo Emerson. "If a man can write a better book, preach a better sermon, or make a better mousetrap than his neighbor, though he builds his house in the woods, the world will make a beaten path to his door." In the business world, it does not matter if you are 1st, 2nd, or 52nd (as Sholes was), or even later (as Remington was). If you can take something already in existence, whether it is a mousetrap or a camera, and make it better than anyone else has made it, customers will come calling.

George Parker

Parker Pens have been used by world leaders to sign important documents. These pens were used by Soviet leader Mikhail Gorbachev and former U.S. President Ronald Reagan to sign the INF Treaty.

George Parker was another businessperson who would have vouched for the truth in Emerson's saying. While teaching at a telegraphy school in Janesville, Wisconsin, Parker tried to make a few extra dollars by selling pens on the side. This part-time job, however, soon proved to be more trouble than it was worth. A man of high principles, Parker believed in servicing what he sold. Unfortunately, the pens he was selling in 1888 leaked badly. Before long Parker was spending so much time repairing leaky pens for customers that he barely found time to prepare his lessons.

Parker decided to build a better pen—one that did not leak. By 1889 he had designed a new version of the simple writing tool. Two years later, he started his own pen company. Parker's nonleaking pens quickly became one of the most popular brands in the world.

This is not a book about pioneers and trailblazers in industry. This book focuses instead on improvers, refiners, and polishers. It is not about the inventor of the camera, but about how George Eastman made a better camera, one that could be used by anyone. The book is about people such as Gillette and Zamboni and their better razors and ice resurfacers. It is about companies such as Pepperidge Farm, Caterpillar, and Otis, and their better bread, heavy equipment, and elevators.

Stuck on the
Ground Floor

Otis Elevators

Most people don't consider an elevator ride a test of courage. We're so used to zipping up and down 50 floors that the worst part of the ride may be having to stand close to a stranger for a few seconds. People are about as worried that an elevator will crash to the earth as they are that a meteor will strike.

That trust in elevators, however, took several decades to form. In Elisha Otis's time, the average person was no more interested in riding an elevator than in walking across Niagara Falls on a tightrope. Otis improved elevators and worked hard to overcome people's fears by demonstrating that his elevator was safe. Before he died, Otis was slowly winning over the public, thereby paving the way for modern skyscrapers.

Opposite: Elevator operators stand in front of a pair of Otis elevators in Davenport, Iowa, during the 1930s.

Elisha Otis was born in 1811. Although he grew up on a farm, he had no interest in raising crops. For a long time, Otis could not seem to get comfortable at any occupation. He built a gristmill in Vermont but did not earn enough money to keep it going. After building carriages for several years, he tried operating a sawmill. Business was no better for Otis than it had been in the old days, however, and he gave up milling for good.

After a brief fling as an inventor and a mechanic, Elisha opened a shop in Albany, New York. He intended to manufacture small machines. His experience with mills had given him respect for the efficiency of water as an energy source, and he planned to power his shop with a water turbine. Bad luck and ill health continued to follow him, though. He had barely begun manufacturing, using water from a stream for power, when the city of Albany claimed the stream for the city's water supply.

The word **manufacture** refers to the making of articles by hand or with machines.

Still looking for a way to use his handyman talents, Otis moved to New Jersey and then to Yonkers, New York, in 1852. He was hired as a master mechanic by the Bedstead Manufacturing Company, which was expanding its business into New Jersey. Heavy, bulky equipment had to be hauled up to the second floor of the firm's new quarters. Otis had to build an elevator that could move the freight safely.

A tinkerer by nature, Otis tried to improve the elevator designs then in use. He noticed that elevators depended too much on a single cable. If

Elisha Otis

that cable snapped, nothing could prevent the whole works from crashing down. Otis thought the system was too risky to lift thousands of pounds of machinery. He looked for a backup system that could prevent disaster if the rope should break.

The device he came up with used a simple wagon spring. The ends of the spring were attached to the top of the elevator platform, while the middle of the spring was connected to the overhead lifting cable. If the cable broke, the tension on the spring would disappear, and the spring would straighten out. Its ends would then catch in ratchets on the side rails of the elevator shaft. The platform would be held in place until a new cable could be attached.

The safety hoist worked well, and the Bedstead Manufacturing Company completed its move with no problems. Otis didn't realize that he might have invented something of value to many people—he merely took satisfaction in a job well done. Then it was time to move on to something else.

Still searching for a successful career, he was impressed by the fabulous tales of the gold strike in the West. As usual, his timing was not good. It was nearly three years after the 1849 gold rush when Elisha finally prepared to take his family to California.

Just before they left, however, he received an urgent summons from businessman Benjamin Newhouse. A cable on a freight hoist at Newhouse's factory had recently snapped, causing a terrible accident. Newhouse had heard about Otis's safety device and wanted it for his factory. Otis agreed to postpone his move to California long enough to install two safety elevators at Newhouse's plant. Before he had finished this job, a picture frame company in the same neighborhood asked if he could build a similar hoist for them.

This sudden interest made Otis realize that he had discovered something extremely valuable. Surely owners of buildings throughout the country would see that enormous effort and countless steps could be saved with his safety elevators. He pictured tall buildings busy with elevator traffic, both freight and passenger. Giving up his dreams of California gold, he organized the E. G. Otis Company in September of 1853.

Once again, however, his business floundered almost as soon as he started it. The initial interest in his safety elevator was followed by silence. Stories of awful elevator accidents were far too common; everyone could imagine the terror of hearing the cable snap, then feeling the elevator fall out from under them. Otis received a few requests from merchants who were willing to trust their goods to the strength of a cable rope. But no one thought it was worth risking human lives just to save a few steps. Otis did not receive any orders for a passenger elevator, and his debts began to pile up.

With his latest enterprise sinking quickly, Otis desperately sought a way to prove his elevator was

Debt is an obligation to pay something, like a bill. Otis was concerned because he was getting a lot of bills. Yet, he wasn't selling enough elevators to make money to pay those bills.

Otis thrilled people at the American Institute Fair in 1854 by having an assistant cut the rope that supported the elevator platform upon which he stood.

One way to overcome people's fear or distrust of a product is to **demonstrate**, or show, how it works. When people can actually see a product doing what it was meant to do, they are more likely to use or buy that product. Demonstrations are also a way for sellers to make people more familiar with products.

safe. The chance came in 1854 when the American Institute Fair allowed him to set up a demonstration in the main exhibition hall of New York's Crystal Palace. Otis set up the most dramatic situation he could think of: elevator accidents with himself aboard!

He built a large elevator in the hall. For the demonstration, he stepped onto the elevator platform and had it lifted four stories above the watching crowd. An assistant cut the cable, and the platform plummeted toward the ground. The onlookers gasped and screamed in horror. Then Otis's safety device brought the elevator to a quick halt in midfall.

Repeated demonstrations of Otis's safety device slowly overcame the public's suspicion of elevators. He installed 15 elevators in 1855 and 27 the following year, all of them designed to handle freight and not people. In 1857 he was asked to construct the world's first safety passenger elevator in a five-story china store in New York City.

Few merchants, however, were willing to follow the china store's lead. Otis attracted just enough business to keep his company going. At the time of his death from diphtheria in 1861, passenger elevators were still a novelty. The E. G. Otis Company employed only a few workers, and his entire business was judged to be worth $5,000.

Elisha's sons, Charles and Norton, continued his pioneering efforts. They were not only good mechanics, like their father, but good businessmen.

An illustration of the Otis Brothers Safety Elevator for Freight in the 1860s

A **patent** is the exclusive right to own, use, and dispose of an invention. The U.S. Patent Office issues more than 1,200 patents each week.

They invented more than 50 patented features, including elevator brakes in 1864. They installed the first Otis electric elevator in 1889. When engineering breakthroughs in the late 19th century triggered the construction of skyscrapers, passenger elevators became a profitable item. Such buildings as the Washington Monument (built in 1888) and high-rise hotels contained elevators.

Although it took a little longer than usual for people to beat a path to Otis's door, the elevator boom proved that Elisha Otis's elevator improvement was an idea worth more than a gold mine.

Workers assemble folding Kodak cameras in the early 1900s.

The Ordeal of Photography

Eastman Kodak Company

"Do you mind if I take your picture?" That question is now asked as a matter of courtesy with respect to privacy. But there was a time when it was a very serious question, for reasons that had more to do with endurance than with privacy.

On a trip to Mackinac Island, Michigan, in the 1870s, George Eastman asked a group of tourists to pose for a picture. The amount of equipment involved and the slowness of the process meant that, even in the hands of a professional, they would be sacrificing more than a few minutes of their time. With Eastman, an amateur, setting up the picture, it took half an hour of standing under a blazing sun. The tourists put up with the hardship, expecting their efforts would be rewarded with a

Researchers at Kodak's synthetic chemicals research facility look for new and better ways to make Kodak products. Eastman Kodak Company recognized the value of research and development early, opening its first laboratory in 1912.

copy of the photograph. Little did they know that Eastman was thinking only of getting a picture for his own collection. When he merely thanked them and sent them on their way, they were enraged.

It was not the first time Eastman had thought there must be a better way to take photographs. Eventually, this bank teller, completely untrained in either science or photography, found a better way. It was he who first turned photography from a combination weight-lifting exercise, balancing act, and laboratory experiment into something that children could do simply by pressing a button.

George Eastman was born in 1854 in Waterville, New York. His father taught penmanship and bookkeeping, and had founded the United States' first business school in Rochester, New York, some 12 years earlier. It wasn't until 1860, however, that the elder Eastman felt his school was financially solid enough to risk moving his family to Rochester. Two years later, Mr. Eastman died. George was eight.

George's mother made ends meet for a while by taking in boarders. But as the only son in the family, George was expected to do his part. At the age of 14, he quit school to help support the family. He worked first as a messenger boy for an insurance firm and later as a clerk for a Rochester Bank. Eastman was neat and thrifty. He always kept careful watch over his money and saved much of his modest wages.

When he was 24, Eastman decided to treat himself to his first vacation. While making plans to travel to the Caribbean Sea, he began to outfit himself with camera equipment so he could bring back pictures of his trip. A few trial runs, however, were enough to discourage him. The thought of carting around all that heavy equipment—glass tanks, a cumbersome camera and tripod, and a dark tent—along with chemicals to process the glass photographic plates, made the effort seem more of a chore than fun and relaxation.

Eastman was so appalled at the nuisance involved in photography that he canceled his trip and instead began to look for a way to make photographic equipment more convenient. After working days at the bank, he would stay up late each night experimenting with glass plates in his mother's kitchen. He often worked at it until he grew exhausted and curled up in a blanket on the floor next to the stove.

Eastman's characteristic attention to detail served

George Eastman at 36

him well as an inventor. Prior to his invention, the manufacture of photographic plates was more of an art than a science. But, by 1879, the Rochester bookkeeper had developed and patented a process that used a machine to spread a gelatin solution uniformly over the glass plates. He began to sell the plates to the public. Although this new process eliminated a lot of guesswork, it was not foolproof, as Eastman learned the hard way in 1880. He had just persuaded one of his mother's boarders to invest money in his project, and had rented a third-floor loft to produce the new plates, when a batch of plates inexplicably went bad.

Eastman realized that if he wanted to be successful in the photographic equipment business, he could no longer afford to treat it as a sideline. He quit his job at the bank and traveled to England to learn more about developing processes. He then worked long hours for his newly formed Eastman Dry Plate Company.

In 1884 Eastman thought of a way to get rid of those temperamental glass plates altogether. He took the first step toward camera simplification when he substituted paper for glass plates.

Eastman tried to persuade his photographic plate customers, mostly professional photographers, to switch over to the new paper-based film. To his astonishment, they did not. Most disliked the image of paper grain that could be seen on the finished pictures. That forced him to focus his efforts on

The Eastman Dry Plate and Film Company in 1889

A **sideline** is a job done in addition to a regular job. While George Eastman relied on his job at the bank for a regular paycheck, he also worked at making Eastman Dry Plate Company a profitable business. Sometimes people operate a business as a sideline to see if they can be successful in that business. If they think they will be successful, then they can quit their regular job and work full time in their own business.

The first Kodak camera, introduced in 1888, sold for $25 and was loaded with enough film for 100 pictures.

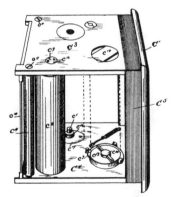

A drawing from Eastman's patent application for the camera pictured above

amateur photographers who, like him, were too exasperated by all the bother to spend much time taking pictures.

Along with replacing glass plates with paper film, Eastman took two more steps to reach his goal of an easy-to-operate photographic process. First, he reduced the bulky camera and its cartload of inconvenient accessories to a single small, reasonably priced, lightweight box. Second, he took the burden of film developing away from the photographer. He accomplished both of these when he introduced a new camera in 1888. For $25, Eastman sold a camera already loaded with a 100-exposure roll of film. When the roll was used up, the customer simply sent the camera back to Eastman, who unloaded the film, developed and printed it, and sent the camera back ready to take another 100 pictures.

EASTMAN KODAK CO.'S BROWNIE CAMERAS $1.00

Make pictures 2¼ x 2¼ inches. Load in Daylight with our six exposure film cartridges and are so simple they can be easily

Operated by any School Boy or Girl.

Fitted with fine Meniscus lenses and our improved rotary shutters for snap shots or time exposures. Strongly made, covered with imitation leather, have nickeled fittings and produce the best results.

Forty-four page booklet giving full directions for operating the camera, together with chapters on "Snap-Shots," "Time Exposures," "Flash Lights," "Developing" and "Printing," free with every instrument.

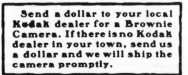

Brownie Camera for 2¼ x 2¼ pictures,	. . . .	$1.00
Transparent-Film Cartridge, 6 exposures, 2¼ x 2¼,	. . . . .	.15
Paper-Film Cartridge, 6 exposures, 2¼ x 2¼,	. . . . .	.10
Brownie Developing and Printing Outfit,	. . . . . .	.75

The Brownie Camera Club.

Every boy and girl under sixteen years of age should join the BROWNIE CAMERA CLUB. Fifty Kodaks, valued at over $500.00, will be given to the members of the club as prizes for the best pictures made with the Brownie Cameras and every member of the club will be given a copy of our Photographic Art Brochure. No initiation fees or dues if you own a Brownie. Ask your dealer or write us for a Brownie Camera Club Constitution.

Send a dollar to your local Kodak dealer for a Brownie Camera. If there is no Kodak dealer in your town, send us a dollar and we will ship the camera promptly.

EASTMAN KODAK CO.
Rochester, N. Y.

Manufacturers will often adopt **brand names** to help customers tell the difference between their product and other manufacturers' products. Kodak is the brand name used by Eastman Kodak Company. Kodak competes with other film manufacturers for all the customers who want to buy film. Kodak hopes that people will buy Kodak film rather than another manufacturer's brand of film. By calling it Kodak film, and then telling people to buy only that film, the company has a better chance of selling to more people than it would if it simply labeled the package "film."

Opposite: An early 1900s advertisement for Kodak's Brownie camera

That same year, Eastman came up with the word *Kodak* as the brand name for his products. The word had no special meaning; it just happened that Eastman liked word combinations that started and ended with the same consonant, and he especially liked the letter *k. Kodak* was chosen strictly for the way it looked and sounded.

In 1889 Eastman introduced a transparent roll film that did not use a paper base. As Eastman had always suspected, there were thousands of people who were interested in taking photographs but had not wanted to use the bulky equipment that was available. By 1896 Eastman Kodak Company, as the company had been renamed, had made more than 100,000 cameras and had shrewdly worked out a series of exclusive sales contracts with distributors.

Yet, despite the improvements he had made, Eastman was far from satisfied. He wanted to make a camera so simple that a child could operate it.

In 1900 Kodak came out with just such a model, the Brownie camera. Selling for one dollar, the camera reduced the complex scientific process of reproducing images to two simple actions: aim the lens and press a button. Not only did the Brownie camera sell well, but it coaxed millions of otherwise timid customers into trying photography. This led to an explosion in sales of camera film and developing services.

Thanks to George Eastman, the joys of photography became available to the most inept amateur.

With an office in St. Petersburg, Russia, in 1910, Eastman Kodak Company did business internationally.

Eastman Kodak Company grew into a giant corporation, and George Eastman had enough money that he could afford to give away millions of dollars to charitable causes before his death in 1932.

By that time, he had provided convincing proof of the wisdom of Ralph Waldo Emerson's theory. He had built a better camera, and not only had the world beaten a path to his door, but they had all but beaten down the doors to purchase it.

The corporation has become the major form of business in the United States. Technically, a **corporation** is an association of individuals allowed by law to use a common name and to change its membership without ending the association. Most people think of a corporation as just a large company, though.

Reinventing
the World

Gillette

KING C. GILLETTE WAS A MAN WITH ambitions grand enough to match his first name. Gillette's goal was to reinvent the world. Among his ideas for building a perfect world, or utopia, was his plan to reorganize the world into a single corporation, with every man, woman, and child an equal shareholder.

His proposals, which he spelled out in an 1894 book called *The Human Drift*, were ignored or laughed at by the public. Stung by the rejection, Gillette settled down to design something a little more workable. Compared with his utopian plans, Gillette's invention of the disposable safety razor seems trivial. But by inventing that razor, Gillette ushered in the era of the disposable society, in which products are used once and thrown away.

A **shareholder** is someone who owns a portion of property, which can be land, business, or anything else of value. A **utopia** is defined as an ideal social system. Gillette proposed that the world should be organized in such a way that every person had the same amount of property.

The first Gillette razor and blade took a long time to develop, but the set was a marked improvement over the straight-edge razors that people had used for ages.

Competition is one of the basic features of the U.S. business system. **Competition** means trying to get something that others are also trying to get. Competition in business can occur in many ways. Producers compete for the best raw materials. Businesses compete with each other for the most customers. Companies compete to make the best-quality or lowest-priced product or service.

While environmentalists and others would argue that this was not a change for the better, the convenience of disposable products has been too attractive for many consumers to resist. Gillette's razor beat the competition so badly that it altered the shaving habits of an entire generation of men.

King Gillette was born in Fond du Lac, Wisconsin, in 1855, and grew up in Chicago, Illinois. Along with his father and two brothers, Gillette considered himself to be an inventor, even though he had little mechanical training or skill. In 1871 a fire destroyed the family's belongings and left the Gillettes destitute. Seventeen-year-old King Gillette then left home to start a fresh life, working first as a clerk, then beginning a career as a traveling salesman when he was 21.

Gillette seemed destined to spend his entire career hawking wares on the road. In 1891 he found a more lucrative sales job with the Baltimore Seal Co. under the direction of William Painter. Painter was an inventor who had struck it rich by developing an improved bottle cap. When he learned that Gillette was also interested in inventing, he offered his salesman some advice. According to Painter, a smart inventor should work at designing a product that, like his bottle cap, would be used once and then thrown away. That way there would always be a demand for the product.

Gillette thought about Painter's advice, but continued to pursue his utopian dreams. When *The*

Human Drift turned out to be a failure, he began a structured search for the perfect thing to invent. He started with the letter *A* and went through the entire alphabet, trying to think of a product to make. It was not until 1895 that inspiration struck.

While shaving at his Brookline, Massachusetts, home, Gillette found that the blade of his razor had grown dull. Even in the best of times, a razor blade was a nuisance; it had to be stropped, or dragged repeatedly across a leather strap, after each shave. Regular stropping would keep it sharp until it was so dull and deformed that it had to be reground by an expert. This was one of those times, and Gillette didn't want to bother with the process.

Suddenly it occurred to Gillette that he had stumbled on the opportunity he had tried to create. What if a person were to make a blade so small and thin that it cost almost nothing in raw materials? Then he could sell it very cheaply—so cheaply that when the blade got dull, the customer could afford to throw it away and buy a new one. Never again would anyone have to go to the trouble of sharpening a razor blade.

Gillette thought it would be easy to make razors from steel ribbons, a thin type of steel used for making clock springs. But he was speaking as a bottle-cap salesman, not as a mechanical genius. He later admitted that he probably never would have begun the project if he had known anything about razors, and especially about steel. As it was,

King Camp Gillette

Manufacturers need **raw materials** to make products. For Gillette, the raw material for his razor blade was steel, which he had to shape into blades.

he bought some basic tools and began working on steel ribbon.

Before long Gillette realized that his project was not as easy as he had thought. Frustrated, he talked with expert toolmakers and scientists, who told him two things. First, that no one could make a decent razor blade out of steel ribbon; he would need to use quality steel. Second, he shouldn't bother with buying quality steel because the whole idea was a waste of time and money.

A business with two or more owners, or partners, like the company that Gillette formed with William Nickerson, is called a **partnership**. A business owned by just one person is called a **sole proprietorship**. Large companies with many owners are called **corporations**.

Although his obsession with creating a disposable blade caused many friends to tease him, Gillette refused to give up. Then, in 1901, a friend described Gillette's effort to a machinist named William Nickerson. At first, Nickerson, a graduate of the prestigious Massachusetts Institute of Technology, thought little of the idea of disposable blades. But eventually he agreed to join Gillette as a partner in the venture, which became the American Safety Razor Company. It was Nickerson who designed the tools and machines that produced the thin razor blades. In 1903, after two years spent perfecting every step of the process, Nickerson finally was satisfied. He had done what Gillette had spent eight years trying to do: make a thin blade hard enough, sharp enough, and straight enough to give a good shave.

Gillette Safety Razor Company, as it had been renamed in 1902, began manufacturing its products during 1903 in a small loft over a Boston fish shop.

No. 775,134.

PATENTED NOV. 15, 1904.

K. C. GILLETTE.
RAZOR.
APPLICATION FILED DEC. 3, 1901.

NO MODEL.

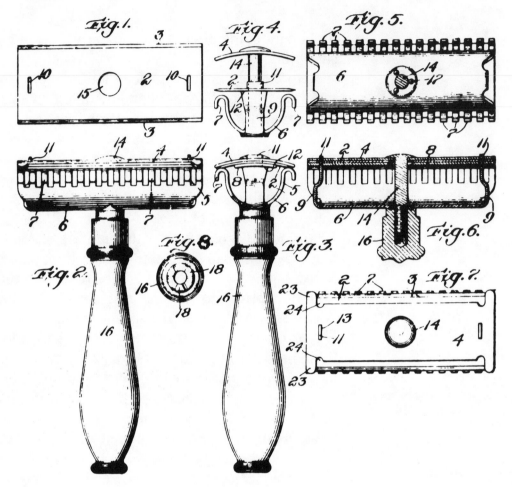

Witnesses:
Ruby M Banfield
Margaret A Damon

Inventor:
King C Gillette,
by
E. S. Chadwick,
Attorney

*Opposite: A drawing
from the patent granted to
Gillette for his razor*

A person who gives money
or something else of value
to a business with the expec-
tation of getting the money
back with a little extra if the
business is successful is
called an **investor**. Every
new business requires an
initial investment of some
amount of money.

The razor set, which was sold for five dollars,
was a metal handle and 20 waferlike, single-edged,
disposable blades. He also sold packages of replacement blades.

Gillette's customers were satisfied, and word
began to spread about this new shaving tool. Yet
Gillette Safety Razor Company sold only 51 razor
sets and 168 replacement blades during its first year
in business. Gillette realized he could never make
enough razors and blades in the cramped loft to
break even, much less amass the fortune he had
hoped to make. Yet he did not have enough money
to expand his facilities.

The problem was solved when a Boston investor,
John Joyce, came forward with $60,000. With those
funds, and having received a patent from the
government, Gillette purchased a six-story building
in South Boston. Before long he was turning out
shaving products with a vengeance and was selling
all he could make. The figures illustrate the
suddenness with which United States men changed
their shaving habits. In 1904, his second year of
operation, Gillette sold more than 90,000 razors
and 123,000 blades. Razor sales tripled in 1905, and
sales of razor blades were nearly 10 times the 1904
total.

William Painter's advice to Gillette began to pay
dividends in the next years. While sales of the
permanent razor handles began to level off, sales of
the throwaway portion, the blades, kept soaring.

Gillette received a big boost when U.S. troops began using Gillette razors during World War I.

As if this booming company needed any further stimulation of sales, World War I provided it with an even larger market. Soldiers spending weeks in the trenches found it made far more sense to use disposable blades than to try to keep a razor sharp. The United States government put in orders for millions of razors and blades. By the war's end, Gillette Safety Razor Company was selling hundreds of millions of blades a year. Even more importantly, an entire generation of men had grown used to shaving with disposable blades. The day of the barber shave and the permanent razor was quickly drawing to a close.

King Gillette, however, did not stay around to preside over his empire. His reign lasted only until 1910, because of continual disputes with his chief backer, John Joyce. Joyce bought out the company's founder for slightly less than a million dollars, far less than Gillette could have made had he kept a financial interest in the company. Even so, Gillette retained the title of company president until 1931. But the money he received from Joyce was enough to allow the former bottle-cap salesman to get back to his more important work, reforming society.

That monumental task was left for others to accomplish when Gillette died in California in 1932. Although his intentional efforts for reform never amounted to anything, he discovered in traveling that he had unintentionally altered life on this planet. He had seen men using his blades throughout the world, from the northernmost towns of Norway to settlements in the Sahara Desert.

Photograph provided by Roll-Royce Motor Cars Inc.

A Mechanic's Car

Rolls-Royce Motor Cars

T HE AUTOMOBILE INDUSTRY HAS AL-
ways been thrilled by excellence in design. The
best-designed cars have traditionally come from
Europe. A German engineer, Rudolph Diesel, won
lasting fame and brief fortune with his improved
version of the internal combustion engine. Patented
in 1892, it proved to be three times as efficient as
any engine previously on the market.

The strongest claim to European superiority in
the manufacture of automobiles has been that of
the British firm, Rolls-Royce Motor Cars Limited.
For more than 85 years, it has been highly regarded
for luxurious, precision-crafted automobiles. The
very mention of Rolls-Royce sparks visions of royalty,
mansions, sprawling estates, and bottomless bank
accounts.

The man who created the company was no well-bred English lord, however, but a poorly educated, working-class mechanic. While his cars took on a snobbish air as toys that only the richest people could afford, Royce was known to sign his name "Henry Royce, mechanic" long after he became famous.

Henry Royce was born in 1863, the son of a poor miller. His father died when Henry was 10, and the lad was sent off to make his own way in the world. After hustling newspapers and running errands for money, he was apprenticed to a railroad locomotive shop. As an apprentice, he was obliged to pay a fee to learn the trade. But his money ran out before he could complete the training, and he had to take a job with a toolmaker.

While working full time at that job, he tried to increase his chances of finding other work by attending night school. Taking classes on electricity, he mastered the subject well enough to go into business for himself. In 1884, when Royce was 21, he began building electrical cranes with a partner. He formed F. H. Royce, Ltd. in 1894.

Royce was both a perfectionist and a workaholic. He was frequently so absorbed in his work that he forgot to eat. While such habits did little for his health, they did enable him to produce exceptional products. His business grew steadily until, in 1902, he felt secure enough to reward himself by purchasing a two-cylinder automobile.

In the 19th century, a young person often became an **apprentice** to a skilled worker to learn a skill or trade like blacksmithing. The apprentice worked for little or no money but gained experience. Sometimes apprentices had to pay a fee for the apprenticeship. Today, most people go to a college, university, or vocational school to learn a skill.

Photograph provided by Rolls-Royce Motor Cars Inc.

Henry Royce

Most people at that time would have been thrilled to own any car, let alone a Decauville, the respected model that Royce had bought. But what was good enough for others was not good enough for Royce, the master mechanic. In Royce's mind, rattling, vibration, worn parts, and mechanical malfunctions were not just inconvenient. They were offensive—signs that someone had not taken the time to design or build the product correctly.

It may be that only Henry Royce could have built a car to satisfy him. Setting aside a part of his electrical shop, he began to build an automobile the way he thought one ought to be built.

All Royce did was use the very best materials, find the best way to put them all together, and then build the car as well as it could possibly be constructed.

On April 1, 1904, he finished his two-seater. The most remarkable feature of his car was that it ran very quietly and smoothly. Royce had so carefully balanced all the parts of the engine that there was almost no vibration. The moving parts were fitted so precisely that, even after a long period of use, they showed almost no wear. With his knowledge of electricity, Royce also included a more reliable electrical system and spent a considerable amount of time improving the carburetor.

Although some people considered his automobile too heavy for its size, Royce was so pleased with his finished product that he built two others for friends.

That is probably as far as he would have gone in building cars had he not met Charles Rolls. Royce, after all, was not suited for selling expensive cars. Not only did he lack contacts among the wealthy people who could afford a car, he was also a shy, stubborn man who disliked strangers. He would not even travel to London for a meeting with Rolls, the wealthy and influential son of an English baron.

Fortunately for him, Rolls swallowed his pride and came to Royce. Rolls, born in 1877, had the money to indulge his fascination with the newly developed cars. He had built a reputation as an automobile racer and as one of his country's first airplane pilots. Aware that rank had its privileges, he routinely ignored the country's speed limit on automobiles and apparently was never prosecuted for it.

Rolls had been looking for a British-made automobile that could match the quality of the expensive French and Belgian models he was selling at his London dealership. After one look at Henry Royce's machine, Rolls knew he had found the car he was looking for. In 1904 he signed an agreement to sell all the cars that Royce could produce. Although Royce was the one making the cars, his young partner had the more influential name, and so the company became known as Rolls-Royce, Ltd.

Royce then began to tailor his cars to the wealthy clients to whom Rolls was selling. The Rolls-Royce became larger, more powerful, and more elegant. In

Photograph provided by Rolls-Royce Motor Cars Inc.

Charles Rolls

A **dealership** is a store or other sales agency which is authorized by a company, such as a car manufacturer, to sell its product.

The Silver Ghost has been called the best built car in the world.

Rolls-Royce got its start at this Cook Street factory in Manchester, England.

1907 Royce came out with what many automobile historians consider the best car ever produced. This six-cylinder vehicle was dubbed the "Silver Ghost" because of its almost noiseless engine and its shiny aluminum and silver-plate finish.

The perfectionist in Royce was obvious in the construction of this car. The crankshaft bearings, for example, had to be ground within 1/4,000 of an inch of specifications. The result was a silent, silky-smooth ride in a virtually indestructible framework. Of the 7,876 Ghosts manufactured from 1907 to 1926, half are still in operation. The original Silver Ghost was still running quietly after 500,000 road miles (804,500 kilometers)!

An illustration of Henry Royce in the Cook Street factory

The success of the Silver Ghost forced Royce to move into a larger factory. But while other automobile manufacturers were switching to assembly lines to cut production costs, Rolls-Royce continued to build a limited number of superior-quality motor cars.

Charles Rolls did not have long to enjoy the prestige of the car that bore his name. He was killed in an airplane crash in 1910—the first Englishman to die in an aviation accident. Henry Royce collapsed from the burden of his enormous work load and his poor health habits in 1911. He moved to France to recover his health. Although he continued to direct operations of the company, he rarely returned to the factory.

It costs money to make products. In addition to buying the raw materials to make something, businesses have to pay workers involved in production. They have to pay for energy used in manufacturing. All of those expenses make up the **production costs**.

In the years since, the company has not always performed up to its expectations as a class act. During the 1960s and early 1970s, the firm miscalculated in an attempt to design a superior jet engine. Each engine cost a quarter of a million dollars more than had been estimated. The firm went bankrupt in 1971 and was forced to reorganize. Now two English companies bear the Rolls-Royce name. Rolls-Royce PLC manufactures jet engines and other aerospace and industrial turbine products. Rolls-Royce Motor Cars Limited builds Rolls-Royce and Bentley motor cars. Both companies are flourishing and are regarded as making the finest products in their fields. The name Rolls-Royce lives on as a symbol of high quality.

A company or individual goes into **bankruptcy** when they cannot pay their debts. A company that goes bankrupt either goes out of business or reorganizes. When a company reorganizes, as Rolls-Royce did, it comes up with a plan to repay debts while returning the company to a profit-making business.

Track-type tractors, like this one built by The Holt Manufacturing Co., give drivers more power than traditional tractors. They were used mainly for pulling farm implements in the late 1800s and the early 1900s.

Machines for Farm and Road

Caterpillar

THE BATTLE THAT RAGED BETWEEN two turn-of-the-century heavy-equipment manufacturers in California illustrates the fact that a superior product in itself isn't a guarantee of success. By the time an inventor gets his or her product on the market, someone else may have already come up with something better.

For years the firms founded by Daniel Best and Benjamin Holt engaged in a nonstop struggle of one-upmanship. Each new machine they developed had to be updated with more and more features just to keep pace with the latest breakthrough by the other. By the time the two companies merged into the giant Caterpillar Tractor Co. in 1925, they had built up a large inventory of some of the most clever, most rugged heavy machinery in existence.

The products a manufacturer has on his or her property are referred to as **inventory**.

47

It all started in 1859 when Daniel Best decided that farm life was not for him. Like so many young fortune seekers of the time, he dreamed of striking it rich in the gold fields of California. So, he left his home in Iowa and made the rugged trip over the Oregon Trail.

Best spent the next 10 years searching for his fortune. During that time, he supported himself by hunting and by working at a saw mill. But finally he had to face the fact that he was wasting his life chasing after gold. Eventually, he joined a brother who had established a ranch in California.

Best made his move into machinery manufacturing in 1871. While working on his brother's ranch, Best discovered that farmers in the huge, widely scattered fields of the West faced problems unknown to eastern farmers. With so much more ground to cover, there was a great need for increased mechanization. In addition, the expense of transporting crops to processing centers and to markets was a huge burden for farmers.

Best eased one of these problems in 1871 by inventing a grain cleaner that separated grain from straw and other waste right in the field. This saved the money needed to bring it to a cleaning facility. After obtaining a patent for it, Best set up factories in Oregon and in Oakland, California, to make more grain cleaners. They became so popular that Best ran out of space in his production plant and, in 1886, bought a new, larger factory.

In the meantime, Benjamin Holt had pulled up roots in New Hampshire to join an older brother, Charles, in California. Charles had arrived in San Francisco during 1863 and had set up a hardwood-lumber import business. He had initially enjoyed no better luck in this new state than Best had. Benjamin supplied Charles with goods through the Holt brothers' lumber products factory in Concord, New Hampshire.

It was a costly process to cut lumber in Ohio, haul it to the East to be cured and shaped into wheels and axles, and then ship it around the southern tip of South America to San Francisco. Yet after all that effort, many of the wheels dried out and broke down in the hot California sun. The Holt brothers decided to eliminate this problem by manufacturing their own wheels in Stockton, California, from California trees. In 1883 Benjamin Holt moved west to run the new business, Stockton Wheel Company. The company prospered and gradually began to manufacture other types of transportation equipment.

The machine that brought Best and Holt into direct competition was a new type of farm equipment that neither invented. In 1885 Best began manufacturing the Best Combine. Holt followed with his own model in 1886. The combines were developed in response to farmers' demands for machines to help them work their vast lands. The first combines were called "traveling combined

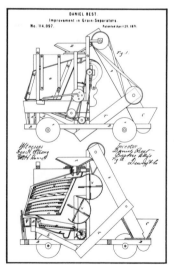

Drawings from Daniel Best's patent application for an improved grain separator

harvester-threshers," a name that was later shortened to combine. Combines were designed to be pulled by horses and made harvesting much more efficient by combining two tasks into one mobile unit.

Best and Holt began to improve both the design of their equipment and the service they offered so their products would stand out from the competition's products. Individually, they built reputations for going right out to the fields to repair any of their products that might have broken down.

Holt's combine featured a breakaway chain belt to combat the problem of runaway horses. The noise from combines often frightened the horses that pulled the machinery through the fields. Holt designed the chain so a link would break if a team of horses bolted suddenly. A new link could be attached in just five minutes, a tremendous savings considering the damage bolting horses could do if they dragged the expensive equipment.

Best then forged ahead in the competition by eliminating horses altogether. His steam-driven harvester, introduced in 1889, opened the way for mechanization in farming. Other steam-driven heavy equipment was quickly brought into production, including a steam traction engine that Holt manufactured the following year. These first self-powered units for farmers were monstrous machines. Some models cut a swath 45 feet (13.5 meters) wide as they rumbled through the fields, supported by wheels that were 15 feet (4.5 meters) wide and 9 feet

Most companies strive to develop an image as reliable, high-quality providers of goods or services. They will frequently offer to service what they sell, which means they will fix it correctly when it breaks. When a company has a good **reputation**, it is likely to have many loyal customers.

Market share refers to the portion of product sales a manufacturer has earned. Best and Holt each sought to increase the percentage of his own product sales among all manufacturers' farm equipment sales combined.

Below: Best's sidehill combine adjusted to allow harvest along hilly slopes.

(2.7 meters) in diameter. Although it is hard to imagine how these machines could be transported economically, Holt and Best expanded their shares of the market by exporting overseas.

For the rest of the 19th century, the farm-machinery industry was buzzing with inventive activity. Again, California farming conditions helped bring about a revolutionary type of product. Ever since the 1850s, farmers around Stockton had worked the area's delta land, which had an especially fertile soil that became heavy and boggy when it was wet. During a period of hard rain, the land became so mucky that people could hardly walk through the mud without sinking up to their knees. Horses were equipped with special shoes to keep them from getting too badly stuck when they worked in the

Employees from Best, left, and Holt Manufacturing Co., right, pose for pictures in front of the company buildings. Daniel Best, sporting a beard and wearing a suit, is seated in the middle of his employees.

wet fields. But the special equipment for these new self-powered machines made them much heavier than normal and harder to steer. Operators of tractors that became stuck faced long days of hard work to free them.

Seeing the problems farmers were having, Benjamin Holt tried to find ways of getting heavy machinery to travel over muddy ground. He was not the first to propose a solution. In fact, by the arrival of the 20th century, more than one hundred patents had been issued to inventors of mechanisms designed to give better traction. Unfortunately, most of these ideas failed miserably.

Holt found the problem just as difficult as his predecessors had. Only after long experimentation and testing did he come up with an answer that satisfied him. On Thanksgiving Day in 1904, Holt demonstrated his latest invention on a swampy section of land outside of Stockton. His machine, riding on an "endless chain of wheels," crawled straight across the mud without a problem.

By 1906 Holt was ready to bring his crawlers into production. By 1910 many of the machines he had built were being used for construction projects in previously unworkable land such as the marshlands of Louisiana and the sands of the Mojave Desert. The tanks that were introduced in World War I were based on Holt's equipment, and many were built by Holt.

Aware that he needed to strive for more improvements in an ever-changing business, Holt then

Below: Holt track-type tractors pulled graders that smoothed road surfaces in the early part of the 20th century.

correctly predicted two trends that greatly contributed to his success. One of these was the conversion of tractors from steam to gasoline. In 1909 Holt moved into the manufacturing plant of a large heavy-equipment company that had gone out of business because it failed to convert its engines to gasoline quickly enough. His second shrewd move was to see a need for better road construction and maintenance equipment because of the growing popularity of automobiles. Holt designed a machine with an adjustable blade that was suspended above a single track—the forerunner of modern snowplows and road graders.

A **manufacturing plant** is a building that contains equipment used in making products and is where products are made.

Best's company had not been idle during this time. Although Dan Best sold out to Holt in 1908, his son, Clarence Best, stayed with the company until 1910. Then, in 1913, the C. L. Best Gas Traction Company, a new company founded by Clarence Best, came out with its own crawler, called the Tracklayer, for fighting through rough terrain.

Eventually, in 1925, these two leading heavy-equipment companies merged into the Caterpillar Tractor Co. Caterpillar now has more than 30 plants operating in the United States and overseas. Some of the better ideas it has developed include graders, concrete pavers, lift trucks, and backhoe loaders. The list certainly will not end there. In the world of heavy equipment, the search for a better machine can never stop.

Caterpillar Tractor Co. was formed as the result of a merger of two different companies. A **merger** is a union of two (or more) companies in which one company buys another. In recent years, mergers (sometimes called takeovers) have become common.

Yesterday's Bread

Pepperidge Farm

Today, most bread is mass-produced. **Mass production** is the production of goods in large quantities. Mass-produced items are each made alike. The jobs necessary to make the product are broken down into small parts, and machines may do most of the work of people.

Whee The Bread Industry Grew from small, local bakeries to large, national baking companies, people grew accustomed to a different flavor of bread. It took the mother of an unhealthy boy to change the industry and provide a better bread.

Mass production came late to the craft of bread baking. Until the early part of the 1900s, bread was baked fresh every day in small amounts by local bakeries. Most people either baked their own bread or bought a loaf or two at the neighborhood store several times a week.

When bread-wrapping machines were developed, a new era swept through the industry. Bread stayed fresh longer. Cars and trucks allowed bakeries to deliver bread and other baked goods far from the home bakery in a short amount of time. Large baking companies began to crowd store shelves with their new national brands.

Bakers tried to gain an edge on each other by cutting costs on ingredients. Many people who remembered the taste of freshly baked bread from their childhood considered these inexpensive national brands tasteless. But by the mid-1930s, bread selection in most stores was limited to these airy, mass-produced breads.

That was the situation in 1937 when Margaret Rudkin began baking. A native of New York City, she had met and married Henry Rudkin when both were working for a stock brokerage firm. While at home raising her family in Fairfield, Connecticut, Rudkin was worried about the persistent health problems of her nine-year-old son. After a doctor suggested that the boy might need a specialized diet, Rudkin became irritated because she could not find any old-fashioned bread. Combing through her files, she dug up several recipes for whole wheat bread.

Like many others at that time, Rudkin had grown used to buying commercial bread. She had never made a loaf of bread in her life, let alone from the coarse, stone-ground, whole wheat flour. She bought top-grade butter, pure molasses, honey, and fresh milk and began developing a recipe of her own.

Rudkin's first efforts nearly sent her scurrying back to the store for bread. Her first loaf came out

Margaret Rudkin

the size and shape of a brick and was just about as hard. But by trial and error she gradually learned the tricks of working with yeast. Before long she was baking bread the way her grandmother had, and her family and friends were loving it.

When Rudkin proudly informed her family doctor that she was baking bread with stone-ground wheat, he seemed skeptical. It seemed to him that she would have to lighten it with white flour to make it appealing to current tastes. Rudkin then brought him a sample. Not only did the doctor like it, he asked for some for both himself and his patients.

Encouraged by these rave reviews, Rudkin tested the market. The six loaves she took to a local grocery store sold quickly. When inquiries came from other grocers, she decided to go into business. Rudkin hired a neighbor girl to help her bake. Within two months, the demand for her superior bread had grown so great that her kitchen became too small. Rudkin had an old stove moved from her basement into a corner of the family's garage and set up operations there. Soon after that, the garage was so overrun that she expanded into the family's polo stable which had stood empty since her husband had suffered a serious riding mishap a few years earlier. The name of her products, Pepperidge Farm, was taken from the family's country home where there were a number of pepperidge trees (sometimes called black tupelo trees).

By this time Rudkin was convinced that the

When Rudkin brought her bread to a local grocer, she was creating a test market. A manufacturer puts a product in a **test market**—producing a small amount and selling in a small area—to see how well it is received by customers. If customers appear to like the product and it sells well, the manufacturer will increase the amount she or he makes and offer it for sale in more places.

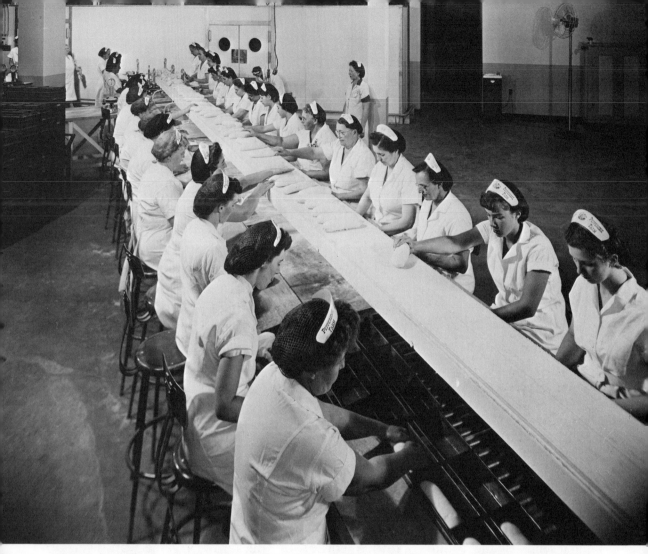

Pepperidge Farm employees knead bread dough. The employees in the background weigh the dough, while employees in the foreground place rolled dough into baking pans.

country was full of people who shared her desire for good old-fashioned bread. It did not seem to matter that the expensive ingredients required her to charge more than twice as much for her loaves as other bakeries were charging for their bread. People were willing to pay for quality. All she had to do was

Controlling the quality of a product is crucial to a business's success. Good quality bread depends on the product's ingredients, the skill of the people making it, and how fast it is delivered.

get grocers and customers to taste it. When she approached the owner of a large New York City grocery store, she came equipped with a loaf of bread and some butter. As she expected, the man did not seem interested in buying her expensive bread, so she cut a slice, buttered it, and handed it to him. He told Rudkin the taste brought back warm memories of homemade bread, and put in an order. Before long he was asking for 200 loaves per day!

At first the Rudkins operated the Pepperidge Farm business as a family project. The three children ran errands and hauled supplies. Henry lugged 25 pounds (11.25 kilograms) of bread with him to drop off with a grocer on his way to his New York City brokerage office. Margaret weighed her dough on baby scales and kneaded it by hand.

Pepperidge Farm's first test kitchen

She hired several more workers, and her success continued. By 1940 Pepperidge Farm was turning out 55,000 loaves per week, far too many to handle as an "in-home" business. Rudkin bought eight delivery trucks and moved into some buildings in Norwalk, Connecticut. Water-operated gristmills ground wheat. Rudkin personally selected the employees for the new bakery, hiring only those who knew nothing about baking bread so she could teach them her way of doing things.

By 1947 Pepperidge Farm had grown so large that Rudkin was able to build a new plant that would employ 160 people. The business that she had started

In more recent times, Pepperidge Farm bakes bread in huge ovens.

in her kitchen without any bread-baking expertise grew into a nationally known brand of products. Margaret Rudkin had turned back the clock on 20th-century progress. By reviving an old method of baking bread, she came up with a product that was remarkably better than any other mass-produced bread of her era.

The Perfect Party Product

Tupperware

Companies that make products usually will back them with a warranty. A **warranty** is a legal document stating that the manufacturer will repair or replace a product if it is found to be defective. While Tupper sold his products with a **lifetime warranty**, most manufacturers back their products with warranties that expire after a certain amount of time.

Earl Tupper had invented a storage container that was better than anyone else's. This container was virtually airtight and watertight, and because it could not be easily damaged, Tupper sold it with a lifetime warranty. If it broke or did not work right, even after years of use, he would replace it. How could a customer go wrong?

Yet several years after Tupper invented his product, no one was beating a path to his door. His food storage containers were sitting on the store shelves gathering dust. It was not until the company got into a party mood that people began to find that there were many tasks for which polyethylene was superior to anything else on the market.

Because Earl Tupper was a man who guarded his privacy well, little is known of his younger years. He was born in 1907 and raised by poor parents in rural New Hampshire. While in his teens, he earned a reputation as an expert salesman for his success at selling his neighbors' fruits and vegetables. But that talent did not mean he was quickly successful in the business world. Tupper worked a variety of self-made jobs, describing himself only as an amateur tinkerer and jack-of-many-trades.

In 1938 the 31-year-old Tupper was shown a block of black material that would change his life. It was polyethylene, a plastic waste product of the oil-refining process. Tupper developed a purifying process that made the hard, smelly material flexible and waterproof. He found that it could withstand hot and cold temperatures. He thought there must be countless uses for a product with those characteristics, if there was a way to mold it into a durable, attractive form.

A waste product is something that is left over after raw materials have been purified or refined.

Believing that plastics were the material of the future, Tupper brainstormed for ways to make use of the polyethylene. Some of his plans, such as a plastic heel for shoes, were too far ahead of their time. But the idea that intrigued him most was the use of polyethylene for an improved food-storage container. Tupper was the first person to discover a way to mold polyethylene without cracking it, and in 1942 he formed his own company to develop products. The plastic was refined into small pellets that were melted and molded into shape. Tupper began selling food-storage containers (his company

Earl Tupper demonstrates a Tupperware® pitcher.

was called Tupper Plastic before 1951) on store shelves in 1945. For many years, he designed all the products himself.

Although pleased with his finished product, Tupper wanted to go a step further to make sure his containers were the best. He researched ways to develop a foolproof, airtight seal on the containers. Eventually, by studying a paint can lid, he found a solution. If the rims of the containers were flared outward slightly, a lid molded to exact dimensions would lock onto it and form an almost airtight seal, provided the air inside was "burped" out. The

patented seal lids were first offered to the public with other Tupper products in 1947.

For some reason, though, whether it was the poor reputation of early plastic products or the difficulty of understanding the idea of burping a container, stores just could not sell Tupperware® products. Tupper, who had established a plant in Farnumsville, Massachusetts, to manufacture his products, wondered why they would not sell.

Sales of Tupper's products soared after the company switched to home party demonstrations in the early 1950s. Now, Tupperware® products are sold exclusively by the home-party method.

Home parties are one way for salespeople to demonstrate their products and get customers to listen to their sales pitches. Door-to-door sales are another way. **Sales techniques** are ways to get customers to notice and, hopefully, buy a product or service.

A person who buys **whole-sale** usually buys a large amount of a product at a greatly reduced price. He or she can then sell the product to other people at a higher price. Most stores people shop at are **retail stores**, which buy goods from wholesale outlets and sell them to customers.

Meanwhile, there were some satisfied customers who were wondering the same thing. A salesman named Tommy Damigella, who had been shown a pink Tupperware® bowl by a friend, thought Tupperware products had great sales potential. At the time, he and his wife were working for Stanley Home Products, which included home-demonstration parties in its sales techniques. Damigella believed that Tupperware® containers were ideal home-party products. He and his wife began buying Tupperware® products wholesale from a distributor and selling them at their own parties. In 1948 the news reached Earl Tupper that there was a salesman who was able to support himself entirely on profits from his Tupperware® sales. The company then began to promote home parties as an alternate method of sales.

In 1949 Tupper received a call from an irate Miami woman about late shipments of her wholesale orders. That woman, Brownie Wise, also had sold for Stanley Home Products until she had received a gift of Tupperware® bowls from a friend. Although it had taken her three days to figure out how to work the seal, she had become so enthused about the product that she had written to Tupper to ask if she could sell his products in homes. A woman with a dynamic personality, Wise had recruited 20 other independent dealers. By the time she called Tupper about shipping delays, she was selling as much as $1,500 worth of Tupperware® products a week.

After listening to Wise's complaints, Tupper realized she was a perfect salesperson for his products. Tupper put Wise in charge of a new home-sales program and, in April 1951, pulled Tupperware® products from the store shelves. The plastic food containers have since been sold exclusively by the home-party method.

Wise's boundless energy and devotion to the product were just what was needed to boost Tupperware® products from a novelty line to something that few modern households could do without. Wise carried Tupperware® samples with her every day to show people; she also carted around a block of polyethylene for the salespeople to rub for good luck. A system was set up by which party hostesses could become dealers, dealers could become managers, and managers could become distributors.

Brownie Wise became a legend at Tupperware® before moving on to become an independent business consultant. When Wise took over the company's sales system, Tupperware® had roughly 200 independent dealers to supplement its trickle of sales from retail stores. Three years later, that number had grown to more than 9,000!

In 1958 the company was rocked by the sudden departure of Wise. Scarcely had things settled down when Tupper sold his business to the Rexall Drug Company. Tupper, who claimed to be disillusioned with the United States, then moved to Costa Rica, where he died in 1983.

Today's Tupperware® products sometimes feature shelves to go along with food storage containers.

Brownie Wise and Earl Tupper, dressed in clothes from a different era, presumably for a company costume party

While the inventor seemed eager to move away from modern United States society, his products had become a familiar part of that society. It has been estimated that as many as 22 million people (almost exclusively women) in the United States attended Tupperware® parties in 1986.

A current sales force that includes more than 89,000 independent dealers in the United States and over 236,000 in 41 other countries proves that even though it got off to a slow start, Earl Tupper's polyethylene product could indeed attract customers.

Two different models of Zamboni machines. The machine on the left is an E-21. The one on the right is a 500 model, the one that is still made today.

The Hottest Machine on Ice

Zamboni Ice-Resurfacing Machines

Frank J. Zamboni

Ice HOCKEY PROMOTERS ADVERTISE their sport as the fastest game on earth. There may be some truth to that claim during the flurries of action when players skate around the ice, slam into each other, and shoot the puck so hard that a spectator cannot always keep track of it. But there is also more waiting time between periods in hockey than in most professional sports. Players and spectators must cool their heels for a full 20 minutes between each 20-minute period.

Had Frank J. Zamboni come on the scene a little sooner, this lull might have been cut short by several minutes. The reason for the long break was originally a strictly practical one. For many years, it took six workers, laboring feverishly with their ice scrapers and hot water hoses, 20 minutes to prepare the ice for another period. By the time Zamboni developed a better way to do it, the 20-minute break was a firmly entrenched tradition and there is little chance that it will change in the near future. Nevertheless, Zamboni's machine has taken the drudgery out of ice resurfacing and has so fascinated anyone who has seen it work that even those who care nothing for ice hockey know the name Zamboni.

Frank Zamboni was born in 1901 and was raised in Idaho. His formal education never advanced beyond the ninth grade. In 1922 the 21-year-old Zamboni moved to California to work with his younger brother in an electrical business. Living outside of Los Angeles near an abundance of dairy farms, the brothers quickly discovered a profitable sideline to their business. Milk producers and consumers in that warm climate were always in need of ice to keep the milk cold and fresh. The Zambonis began producing and selling large quantities of ice and enjoyed a stable business through the Great Depression of the early 1930s.

Later in that decade, however, refrigerators began to replace iceboxes in most homes, leaving the Zambonis with no market for their ice. To salvage their investment in ice-making equipment, the brothers built a skating facility.

The Zambonis actually knew very little about ice rinks. They opened an outdoor rink in January 1940 but installed a roof over it five months later, after giving in to the reality that there was no good way

During the 1930s, the United States suffered through a period called the **Great Depression**. In general, a depression is a period when production and consumption of goods and services slow down. It is a time marked by unemployment and business failures. When a country is suffering from an economic depression, most people do not have much money to live on. During the Great Depression, the U.S. economy was paralyzed. At the height of the Depression, in 1933, about 13 million Americans were out of work. The Depression continued until 1941, when the U.S. entered World War II.

The **market** for ice or any other product or service means the potential buyers for that product.

The Zambonis opened an outdoor ice-skating rink in 1940. Months later, they decided the costs of keeping the rink open under the California sun were too high, so they constructed a building around the ice.

to keep the ice in good shape with the hot California sun shining on it. They settled for a large indoor ice skating surface, 200 feet (60 meters) long and 100 feet (30 meters) wide, which is still in operation today.

The Zambonis soon discovered an unexpected expense with their rink. Even though the surface was nothing but frozen water, it required almost as much maintenance as the most immaculate golf course. Slashing, spinning skates carved deep ruts and holes in the ice, which had to be repaired in order to make skating enjoyable. Zamboni found that it took at least three or four workers an hour and a half of hard labor to resurface the ice.

The most advanced way to clean ice at the time was to attach a large blade to a tractor and drive across the ice. The blade would plane away the rutted surface. Workers would sweep or shovel off the scrapings and then use a hose to add water for a new layer of ice. This seemed like a waste of time and money to Frank Zamboni. In 1942 he began to piece together some equipment in an effort to devise a better system. Starting with war surplus truck axles and a jeep engine, he added more features than were on the standard, plane-dragging tractor. After seven years of adjustments and refinements, Zamboni had developed a fully automated method of resurfacing ice.

His machine was hardly a work of art. It looked very much like what it was, a monstrosity with a

Before there were ice-resurfacing machines, crews had to shovel ice shavings off the surface. Then they had to add more water to make a smooth surface of ice.

Zamboni's first machine looked like what it was—a jeep chassis with a huge wooden box suspended above.

Frank Zamboni, center, works on an early model of what was to become today's Zamboni ice-resurfacer.

huge wooden tank perched on a frame that contained all its equipment. There was a conveyor-belt system to scoop the snowy shavings off the ice, a compartment to store the shavings while the machine was in use, and another built-in system to spray water for a fresh layer of ice. But despite its cumbersome, homemade appearance, Zamboni's machine did the job.

Zamboni considered his ice resurfacer merely a handyman's effort that made his life a little easier; he had no intention of building more machines for sale. But it happened that figure skater Sonja Henie, winner of three Olympic gold medals and 10 world championships, lived in the Los Angeles area. While preparing for one of her professional tours, Henie

The famous figure skater, Sonja Henie, turned out to be a fine spokesperson for Zamboni machines. When Zamboni made a machine for her, she took it on tour with her, where ice rink operators could see it for themselves.

and her supporting cast used Zamboni's ice rink for a practice session. When she saw Zamboni's ice-resurfacing machine in action, Henie was so fascinated by it that she asked him to make one for her.

Zamboni purchased a secondhand jeep and constructed a machine similar to the first one. Unfortunately, Henie had already left on tour by the time it was completed. Since he could not drive the machine to her (under the tremendous burden of its equipment, it could travel at a top speed of nine miles per hour), Zamboni had to take it apart. He loaded the pieces into a trailer that he pulled to St. Louis in the jeep. By the time he arrived there, however, Henie was gone again. Zamboni finally caught up with her in Chicago. There he reassembled the machine, delivered it to Henie, and returned home.

Henie turned out to be the best salesperson Zamboni could have found, and he did not even have to pay her. Wherever the skating star traveled, she brought along Zamboni's machine to resurface the ice. Managers of ice facilities throughout the country saw a free demonstration. Soon Zamboni received a few orders.

At first Zamboni continued to build the machines by hand. But when 10 new orders arrived in 1954, Zamboni formed a company, Frank J. Zamboni & Co., Inc., to continue manufacturing them. It is still not a large company (it employs only 30 to 40 people), but Zamboni makes one of the most widely recognized products in the world. Frank Zamboni's invention has truly drawn the world to his door. By 1988 there were more than 4,000 Zamboni machines in use throughout the world. People in countries like China, the Soviet Union, and South Africa rely on Zamboni machines to keep their ice smooth.

For Further Reading...

Bryant, K.L., Jr. and Dethloff, H.C. *A History of American Business.* Prentice-Hall Inc., 1983.

Clary, D.C. *Great American Brands.* Fairchild Books, 1981.

Fucini, J.J. and Fucini, S. *Entrepreneurs: The Men and Women Behind Famous Brand Names.* G.K. Hall, 1985.

Livesay, H.C. *American Made: Men Who Shaped the American Economy.* Little, Brown & Company, 1980.

Moskowitz, M., Katz, M. and Levering, R., eds. *Everybody's Business.* Harper and Row, 1980.

Slappey, S.G. *Pioneers of American Business.* Grosset & Dunlap, 1970.

Sobel, R. and Sicilia, D.B. *The Entrepreneurs: An American Adventure.* Houghton Mifflin Company, 1986.

Thompson, J. *The Very Rich Book.* William Morrow & Company, 1981.

Vare, E. and Ptacek, G. *Mothers of Invention: From the Bra to the Bomb: Forgotten Women and Their Unforgettable Ideas.* William Morrow & Company, 1988.

INDEX

Words in **boldface** are defined in the text.

J

Joyce, John, 35, 37

K

Kodak, 27, *see also* Eastman Kodak
    Company

L

lifetime warranty, definition of, 61

M

manufacture, definition of, 14
manufacturing plant, definition of, 54
market, definition of, 70
market share, definition of, 51
Massachusetts Institute of
    Technology, 33
mass production, definition of, 55
merger, definition of, 54
Mill, Henry, 9

N

Newhouse, Benjamin, 15-16
New York Crystal Palace, 17
Nickerson, William, 33

O

Otis Brothers Safety Elevator, 18
Otis, Charles, 17
Otis elevators, 11, 13-19
Otis, Elisha, 13-19
Otis, Norton, 17

P

Painter, William, 31, 35
Parker, George, 11
Parker Pen, 11
partnership, definition of, 33
patent, definition of, 19
pens, 11
Pepperidge Farm, 11, 55-60
pepperidge trees, *see* black tupelo trees
photography, 21-28
polyethylene, 61, 62, 66
production costs, definition of, 44
proprietorship, *see* sole proprietorship

Q

quality, 58

R

raw materials, definition of, 32
razors, *see* safety razors
Reagan, Ronald, 11
Remington Arms Co., 10
Remington, Philo, 9, 10
reputation, definition of, 50
retail stores, definition of, 65
Rexall Drug Company, 66
Rolls, Charles, 42, 44
Rolls-Royce Motor Cars, Ltd., 39-45
Rolls-Royce PLC, 45
Royce, Henry, 40-45
Rudkin, Henry, 56, 59
Rudkin, Margaret, 56-60

S

safety razors, 29-37

Tupperware® brand products are a familiar sight in nearly every U.S. home.

ACKNOWLEDGMENTS

The photographs and illustrations in this book are reproduced through the courtesy of: pp. 1, 20, 22, 23, 24, 25, 26, 28, Eastman Kodak Company; pp. 2, 55, 56, 58, 59, 60, Pepperidge Farm; p. 8, Don Urtz/Remington Arms Company, Inc.; p. 10, Remington Arms Company, Inc.; p. 11, Parker Pen USA Limited; pp. 12, 14, 17, 18, Archive, United Technologies Corporation, Hartford, Conn.; pp. 30, 32, 34, 36, The Gillette Company; pp. 46, 51, 52, 53, Caterpillar, Inc.; pp. 61, 63, 64, 66, 67, 80, Tupperware Home Parties; pp. 68, 69, 71, 72, 73, 74, Frank J. Zamboni & Co., Inc.

Cover illustration by Stephen Clement.

ALTERNATOR BOOKS™

INCREDIBLE
TECH
TRIVIA

FUN FACTS AND QUIZZES

Heather E. Schwartz

Lerner Publications ◆ Minneapolis

Lerner Publications Company
A division of Lerner Publishing Group, Inc.
241 First Avenue North
Minneapolis, MN 55401 USA

For reading levels and more information, look up this title at www.lernerbooks.com.

Main body text set in Aptifer Slab LT Pro Regular.
Typeface provided by Linotype AG.

Library of Congress Cataloging-in-Publication Data

The Cataloging-in-Publication Data for *Incredible Tech Trivia Fun Facts and Quizzes* is on file at the Library of Congress.
ISBN 978-1-5124-8332-1 (lib. bdg.)
ISBN 978-1-5124-8339-0 (EB pdf)

Manufactured in the United States of America
1-43339-33159-9/27/2017

CONTENTS

THE INTERNET

Did you know online information has weight? It's true. Downloading a book from the Internet onto a reading device actually makes the device weigh more! So just how heavy is information? Not very heavy, as it turns out. All the information on the Internet weighs only about as much as one strawberry.

Ever wonder how the search engine Google got its name? The number one followed by one hundred zeros is called a googol. Google's inventors liked the sound of that!

Google Searc

Q. What does *http* mean?

A. It stands for hypertext transfer protocol. That's the system used to transmit messages on the Internet.

In which decade was the Internet invented?

A. The 1980s
B. The 1990s
C. The 1960s
D. The 2000s

The answer is C—although back then, the Internet was used only by the US Department of Defense.

Q. **What does *www* mean?**

A. **It stands for World Wide Web. Many people think the World Wide Web is the same thing as the Internet, but it's not. The word *Internet* refers to the communications network that connects computer networks around the world. The term *World Wide Web* refers to the part of the Internet that you can use to find information.**

The country with the highest number of Internet users is

A. China
B. United States
C. Russia
D. Japan

It's A, China. The United States and India follow closely behind.

oogle

I'm Feeling Lucky

You probably know that spam is junk e-mail. But that isn't all it is. Spam is also the name for a canned meat product first sold in 1937.

SPAM
CHOPPED PORK AND HAM
Hormel
Foods

VIDEO GAMES

Some studies show that playing video games can help patients recover from painful injuries. The games distract players while they work to get better.

The first gaming system for home use was the

A. Atari
B. Magnavox Odyssey
C. Nintendo Entertainment System
D. Sony PlayStation

It was B, the Magnavox Odyssey. It was released in 1972, and it hooked up to a TV.

Q. What is the most popular video game of all time?

A. It's *Tetris*. This addictive block-stacking game has sold a whopping 495 million copies.

Q. Why is Pac-Man shaped like a circle with a missing piece?

A. The creator of the game *Pac-Man*, Toru Iwatani, was inspired by a pizza that had a slice taken out.

Ralph Baer was known as the Father of Home Video Games. He learned to fix radios and televisions as a teen and went on to become an engineer. We have his ideas and engineering concepts to thank for modern PlayStations, Xboxes, and Wiis.

Surgeons who play video games at least three hours each week make about 37 percent fewer mistakes in laparoscopic surgery (operations that involve examining the abdomen with a tool called a laparoscope) than those who don't. They also perform the task 27 percent faster.

The first Nintendo game was

A. *Hanafuda*
B. *Donkey Kong*
C. *Mario Bros.*
D. *Pokémon*

The answer is A. And you've probably never heard of it! *Hanafuda* isn't a video game. It's a game played with special cards called *hanafuda*, and it was all the rage in Japan in the late nineteenth century. Nintendo started making *hanafuda* cards back in 1889. It would be quite a while before the company moved on to video games.

SPACE VEHICLES

In 2008 students in the United States were invited to enter a contest to name a Mars rover. Twelve-year-old Clara Ma wrote the winning essay and named the rover *Curiosity*. She also signed her name on the rover before it left Earth.

What was the *Saturn V*?

A. A spacecraft that orbited Saturn
B. A rocket that brought astronauts near enough to Saturn that they could see the planet up close
C. A rocket that brought astronauts to the moon
D. A code name for a flying saucer that NASA considered developing

If you guessed C, you got it. *Saturn V* launched American astronauts to the moon in 1969.

Q. Who was the first person to tweet from space?

A. It was astronaut Michael J. Massimino, who tweeted, "From orbit: Launch was awesome!! I am feeling great, working hard, & enjoying the magnificent views, the adventure of a lifetime has begun!"

Q. What is the fastest spacecraft to launch from Earth?

A. It was a craft called *New Horizons*, which left in 2006 traveling at 36,000 miles (58,000 km) an hour. It was heading to Pluto and finally reached the dwarf planet in 2015.

How do astronauts communicate with their families while traveling in space?

A. Skype
B. Cell phones
C. Softphones
D. Walkie-talkies

They use softphones! These phones work through computer software. Astronauts use a computer's keyboard to dial, they listen through headphones, and they speak through a microphone.

CELL PHONES

If you have a cell phone, you might think the device can do it all—but can it deliver a "smell message"? The oPhone can. This phone, developed by biomedical engineer David Edwards, allows users to choose from a menu of scents and even send their friends a custom-blended smell. How would you like to get a message that smelled like cake and ice cream or sunscreen and ocean air?

Motorola employee Martin Cooper used the very first cell phone to call

A. His wife
B. His mother
C. His brother
D. Another phone company employee

It's D. In 1973 he called Joel Engel, who worked for AT&T, to brag about beating the larger company at developing the phone.

Q. Who invented voice mail?

A. Scott Jones invented it in the early 1990s and earned his company about $50 million. His other inventions include the search engine ChaCha and Gracenote, an Internet music company.

The iPhone is a popular choice among smartphone users. Just how many of these phones have sold over the years?

A. More than one million
B. More than five million
C. More than one billion
D. More than five trillion

C it is! Since the iPhone was introduced in 2007, more than one billion of the devices have been snapped up by consumers. That's a lot of iPhones.

The cell phone is called a cell phone because

A. It is made of cells.
B. It was invented in a prison cell.
C. It works best when callers are in small spaces, or cells.
D. Its transmitters work in a specific area.

The real reason is D. The area where a cell phone's transmitters work is called a cell. At the edge of the cell, the signal strength gets weaker. But another cell will pick up the signal to make it strong again.

ROBOTS

Neil Harbisson is famous for

A. Inventing the world's strongest robot
B. Becoming a cyborg
C. Winning a race against the fastest robot
D. Writing movies about robots

Believe it or not, the answer is B. He became a cyborg, or a person whose brain contains mechanical devices. Harbisson was born able to see only black, white, and gray. But he developed a special antenna that allows him to experience color. In 2004 he had it implanted into his skull.

The word *robot* was first used by a Czech writer in 1921. He used it to describe the mechanical slaves in his play. The Czech word for forced labor is *robota*.

The first surgery performed by a robot took place in

A. 2010
B. 1987
C. 1999
D. 1970

The year was 1987. A robot removed a patient's gallbladder.

Q. When did people start studying artificial intelligence?

A. The term *artificial intelligence* was first used at a conference at Dartmouth College in Hanover, New Hampshire, in 1956. Ever since it's been a formally recognized field of study.

Mind Blown: The first robot was built long ago—*very* long ago. In fact, there is evidence that Egyptians built robotic figures as early as about 3000 BCE! The figures looked like humans and were created to strike a bell on a clock at every hour.

PARO, a robotic seal, is the world's most therapeutic robot, according to *Guinness World Records*. It responds to petting, voice, and light and was specially designed to be cute and cuddly. The robot is used to comfort patients in hospitals and nursing homes.

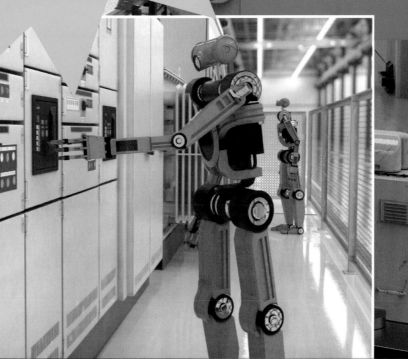

CLOTHING

Technology is an important part of more and more of the clothes being made in recent years. This so-called smart clothing can do so much more than keep you covered. Here's just a sampling of what smart clothing has to offer:

Smart yoga pants help wearers practice yoga. The pants send out vibrations at the hips, knees, and ankles to let those doing yoga know when to move or hold a position.

Smart bikinis tell you when you've been out in the sun too long.

Smart socks for babies send information on the little ones' sleep and breathing patterns straight to their caregivers.

Smart shirts monitor heart rate, breathing, and calories burned.

Smart sleeves track your heart rate and body temperature.

Smart running shorts note your form and coach you to make any necessary adjustments.

Smart jackets give you maps and directions to where you want to be.

CARS

A Klaxon is

A. A type of car
B. A type of car horn
C. A German term to describe a bad driver
D. A German term to describe a pedestrian

The answer is B. Miller Reese Hutchison invented the Klaxon in the early twentieth century. It allowed drivers to aim the sound of the horn at specific pedestrians so they'd know when a car was approaching them.

Q. What is the world's fastest car?

A. According to *Guinness World Records*, the honor of world's fastest car goes to the Thrust SSC. This car's speed was once measured at an amazing 763 miles (1,228 km) an hour.

The first electric car was built in the United States in

A. 1891
B. 1991
C. 2001
D. 2010

Incredibly, the answer is 1891! The car was built by William Morrison in Des Moines, Iowa.

The first car radio was called a Motorola. The name came from combining the words *Victrola*—a brand of phonograph, or record player—and *motor*. Millions of Motorolas were sold following the device's debut in 1930.

The idea for a self-driving car started taking shape centuries before cars were even invented. Around 1500 Leonardo da Vinci (*right*) invented a cart that could move without anyone pushing or pulling it.

CAMERAS

Ever heard of Kodachrome Basin State Park in Utah? It's named after a type of film that was popular in the days when people had to put film in cameras to take pictures. Kodachrome film was known for producing pictures with vibrant colors. The park named for it has bright red rock formations under clear blue skies, so Kodachrome seemed like the perfect thing to call it.

Joseph-Nicéphore Niépce is a big name when it comes to cameras. What is his claim to fame?

A. He invented the video camera.
B. He took the earliest known photograph.
C. He banned cameras in France during the nineteenth century.
D. He invented the instant camera.

The answer is B. Niépce is known for inventing the process to create a permanent photographic image. He captured the view from his window in about 1826, becoming the first person to ever take a picture.

Q. When was the digital camera invented?

A. It was invented in 1975 by Steven Sasson, an engineer who worked for the photography company Eastman Kodak.

Cameras in the nineteenth century were so slow in taking photos that people wore neck braces to help them hold still! If they moved even a little, the picture would come out blurry.

Q. How big is the world's smallest camera?

A. So far, the tiniest one is no bigger than a grain of salt. It's meant for use in surgeries and internal examinations.

In 1912 Donald J. Bell and Albert S. Howell invented a camera made of metal for showing films in movie theaters. This wasn't the first camera made by the two men, though. What do you think their earlier cameras were made of?

A. Wood and leather
B. Plastic
C. Ceramic
D. Crushed stone

They were made of wood and leather. Bell and Howell were inspired to make a metal version of their camera later, when they learned that one of their cameras was ruined by termites and mildew when someone took it on a trip to Africa.

TELEVISION

The very first live international TV broadcast wasn't that exciting.
It was an image of a flag in Andover, Maine.

When was the first wireless TV remote control invented?

A. 1955

B. 1975

C. 1995

D. 2005

Wireless remotes go back to 1955, when a device called the Flash-Matic came on the scene. Even before that, some TV sets came with remotes—but they were connected to the television with a long cord.

Have you ever heard anyone call a remote control a clicker? Ever wonder why they call it this? The term goes back to the Space Command, a kind of remote control introduced by the Zenith company in 1956. The remote operated when tiny hammers struck metal rods, making a clicking noise.

Q. Is it true that sitting too close to a TV can ruin your eyes?

A. No. It might cause eyestrain, but it won't cause any permanent damage to your sight.

Who was Philo T. Farnsworth?

A. The first major TV star
B. The inventor of the television
C. The owner of the most TV sets in the world
D. The first person to ever own a television

Farnsworth was the inventor of the television. He started brainstorming ideas about how to use electricity to transmit images when he was still in high school in the early twentieth century.

TV viewers haven't always been able to watch live events as they unfolded far away. Before 1962 viewers were out of luck if they wanted to watch a live event taking place across the ocean. But that year, the *Telstar 1* satellite was launched. This technological wonder made it possible to send and receive TV signals internationally. Next time you hear the phrase "Live, via satellite," you'll know you have *Telstar 1* technology to thank.

NANOTECHNOLOGY

Q. What exactly *is* nanotechnology?

A. It's the study of microscopic matter between 1 and 100 nanometers. To give a better idea of how small that is: a sheet of paper is about 100,000 nanometers thick!

The word *nano* comes from a Greek word for

A. None
B. Tiny
C. Dwarf
D. Little

If you guessed C, you're right! The Greek word for dwarf is *nanos*.

A nanometer is a unit of measurement equal to

A. Half an inch
B. Half a meter
C. One millionth of a meter
D. One billionth of a meter

The answer is D, one billionth of a meter. That's a really small unit of measurement—but believe it or not, it isn't the smallest. That would be the Planck length, which equals about a millionth of a billionth of a billionth of a billionth of a centimeter across.

Nanorobots can travel through the bloodstream to deliver medications.

Q. What are nanowhiskers?

A. No, they're not whiskers on a tiny cat! They're extremely small fibers that are embedded in fabrics like cotton or linen. They're used to make the fabric waterproof.

Nanorobots can also clean up oil spills.

Gold nanoparticles can be used to kill cancer cells.

Mind Blown:

Six million nanotechnology workers will be needed throughout the world by 2020, according to the National Science Foundation. And the demand for such workers after 2020 seems likely to be even greater. Want to work in nanotechnology? Take plenty of math and science classes and do well in school. A college degree in STEM (science, technology, engineering, or math) should help you on your way.

FOOD

In today's world, tech touches every part of life—even your food. So would you eat . . .

A hamburger grown in a lab? Dutch scientists first served lab-grown meat in 2013.

The package (that's right—the package!) that your favorite snack food comes in? Researchers have discovered that a milk protein can be used to make food wrappers we can eat. Since the packaging is edible, there's no waste left behind after you finish off those crackers or that energy bar. Someday, eating food packaging may not seem weird at all.

The same drink over and over instead of breakfast, lunch, or dinner? Soylent, named for a food in the science fiction novel *Make Room! Make Room!*—on which a famous film called *Soylent Green* is based—is an inventor's solution to food. It's made of only the nutrients the body needs to survive.

24

Pizza made of printed ingredients? It's actually possible to print all kinds of food on special 3-D printers. Running low on your favorite kind of ice cream? Just print out more of that rocky road or mint chocolate chip!

Eggs that don't come from chickens— or from any other animal? They're lab produced instead. And they don't have a yolk! These eggs aren't out on the market just yet, but the company developing them hopes to get them on your breakfast table soon.

MUSIC

The oldest known musical instruments are flutes that are about forty-three thousand years old. Made of bird bone and mammoth ivory, the ancient flutes were discovered in Germany.

Q. Which travels faster, sound waves or light waves?

A. Compared to light waves, sound waves are slow. The speed of sound is about 1,115 feet (340 m) a second. The speed of light is more than 984 million feet (300 million m) a second.

Andy Hildebrand is famous for

A. Inventing many musical instruments
B. His singing voice
C. Inventing Auto-Tune
D. His large music collection

Hildebrand is the inventor of Auto-Tune. He created his real-time pitch correction technology in 1996.

The piano is a

A. String instrument
B. Percussion instrument
C. Keyed zither
D. All of the above

It's D, all of the above! A piano's sounds are made by strings, making it a string instrument. But those strings make sounds because small hammers strike them, making it a percussion instrument. And technically speaking, music experts classify the piano as something called a keyed zither—although they wouldn't disagree that it fits into both the string and percussion categories.

Q. How can you get rid of an earworm?

A. You know those songs that just keep playing in your head . . . over . . . and over . . . and over? Those are earworms. So what can make them stop? Researchers have found that chewing gum after hearing a catchy song might do the trick. Chewing is thought to disrupt the brain's memory for music. No guarantees that this will work for you—but, hey, it's worth a shot!

TRUE OR FALSE

Think you know all there is to know about tech after reading this book? Test yourself by answering these true-or-false questions. The answers are listed at the bottom of page 29— but don't peek!

1. The term *nanotechnology* was first used in 1999.

2. Before the car horn was invented, drivers in Britain had to have someone walk ahead of them waving a red flag and blowing a horn.

3. The singer Cher is usually credited with introducing Auto-Tune to the world.

4. The first computer mouse was developed in 1980.

5. Robots work as shepherds in Australia.

6. A Hollywood movie star helped invent Wi-Fi.

7. The videophone was invented in 2000.

8. One of the first two people to earn a PhD in computer science was a nun.

1) False. A Tokyo professor first used the term in 1974. 2) True. Modern car horns are so much more convenient! 3) True. Cher used the technology in her 1998 hit song "Believe." 4) False. Two Canadian inventors developed a computer mouse in 1952. 5) True. They are programmed to herd cattle, sheep, and other livestock. 6) True. Film star Hedy Lamarr helped craft technology during World War II that kept radio signals from jamming, and the discovery eventually factored into the development of Wi-Fi. 7) False. Videophone technology dates back to 1970. 8) True. Sister Mary Kenneth Keller earned her degree in 1965.

WHO KNEW!?

Trivia about trivia is just as mind-blowing as trivia about tech! Wow your friends with these bits of trivia about trivia itself.

- January 4 is National Trivia Day in the United States.

- The singular form of the word *trivia* is *trivium*—although, according to the dictionary, there's nothing technically incorrect about using the word *trivia* to refer to just one piece of trivia.

- There are more than fifty special editions of the game Trivial Pursuit, with trivia questions focused on *Star Wars*, Power Rangers, country music, and many other topics.

- Trivial Pursuit has been sold in twenty-six countries and at least seventeen languages.

- Spelling counts in trivia. In 2013 twelve-year-old Thomas Hurley was set to win big on the trivia game show *Jeopardy!* Unfortunately, he spelled his final answer wrong, and the judges ruled against him.

SOURCE NOTE

8 Lily Norton, "8 Surprising Space Shuttle Facts," *Space.com*, June 30, 2011, https://www.space.com/12127-8-surprising-space-shuttle-facts.html.

FURTHER INFORMATION

Blakemore, Megan. *All about Smart Technology*. Mankato, MN: North Star Editions, 2017.

Brain POP: Robots
https://www.brainpop.com/technology/computerscience/robots/

NASA Kids' Club
https://www.nasa.gov/kidsclub/index.html

National Geographic. *Quiz Whiz 6: 1,000 Super Fun Mind-Bending Totally Awesome Trivia Questions*. Washington, DC: National Geographic, 2015.

Schwartz, Heather E. *Incredible Science Trivia: Fun Facts and Quizzes*. Minneapolis: Lerner Publications, 2018.

Time for Kids editors. *Time for Kids Big Book of Why*. New York: Time, 2016.

PHOTO ACKNOWLEDGMENTS

The images in this book are used with the permission of: iStock.com/anna1311, p. 4; iStock.com/Prykhodov, pp. 4–5; iStock.com/EllenMoran, p. 5; iStock.com/ilbusca, p. 6; iStock.com/ilbusca, pp. 6–7; iStock.com/londoneye, p. 7 (top); iStock.com/Serdarbayraktar, p. 7 (bottom); iStock.com/ClaudioVentrella, pp. 8–9; © Dmitryzimin/Dreamstime.com, p. 8; iStock.com/suriyasilsaksom, p. 9; Maxx-Studio/Shutterstock.com, pp. 10–11; iStock.com/adventtr, p. 10; iStock.com/Leszek Kobusinski, p. 11; iStock.com/PhonlamaiPhoto, pp. 12–13; iStock.com/PhonlamaiPhoto, p. 12; iStock.com/3alexd, p. 13; iStock.com/darkscott, p. 14; Ian Allenden/Alamy Stock Photo, p. 15 (top); iStock.com/pattonmania, p. 15 (bottom); iStock.com/XXLPhoto, pp. 16-17); iStock.com/Grassetto, p. 16; iStock.com/pictore, p. 17; iStock.com/lechatnoir, pp. 18-19; iStock.com/dimatlt633, p. 18; iStock.com/vladyk, p. 19 (top); iStock.com/jgroup, p. 19 (bottom); iStock.com/saknakorn, p. 20-21; iStock.com/popovaphotop, p. 20; janniwet/Shutterstock.com, p. 21;iStock.com/luchschen, pp. 22–23; SmileStudio/Shutterstock.com, p. 22; iStock.com/monkeybusinessimages, p. 23; iStock.com/mozcann, p. 24 (top); iStock.com/duckycards, p. 24 (bottom); iStock.com/buyit, p. 25 (top); iStock.com/GlobalP, p. 25 (bottom left); iStock.com/L_Shtandel, p. 25 (bottom right); iStock.com/tiler84, pp. 26–27; iStock.com/axstokes, p. 26; Serhiy Kobyakov/Shutterstock.com, p. 27.

Front cover: iStock.com/Rawpixel; iStock.com/inhauscreative;

iStock.com/Kirillm; iStock.com/doomu; R-studio/Shutterstock.com;

Rashad Ashurov/Shutterstock.com.